MW00366158

TWINS

I N S

T W

Essays by Ruth and Rachel Sandweiss

Photographs by David Fields

Running Press

PHILADELPHIA · LONDON

A Running Press ® Miniature Edition™

Photography ©1998 by David Fields

Text © 2000 by Ruth and Rachel Sandweiss

All right reserved under the Pan-American and
International Copyright Conventions

Printed in China

*This book may not be reproduced in whole or in part,
in any form or by any means, electronic or mechanical,
including photocopying, recording, or by any information
storage and retrieval system now known or hereafter
invented, without written permission from the publisher.*

*The proprietary trade dress, including the size and format,
of this Running Press Miniature Edition is the property of
Running Press. It may not be used or reproduced without
the express written permission of Running Press.*

Library of Congress Cataloging-in-Publication Number
00-135509

ISBN 0-7624-0979-7

This book may be ordered by mail from the publisher.
Please include $1.00 for postage and handling.
But try your bookstore first!

Running Press Book Publishers
125 South Twenty-Second Street
Philadelphia, Pennsylvania 19103-4399

Visit us on the web!
www.runningpress.com

Dedications

To twins, our family, and God, who created all this mystery, marvel, and love.

Our deepest thanks to our family—our parents, Samuel and Sharon, who have been a source of constant love and ever-willing support; Beth and Judy, close confidantes whose sisterly love has kept us smiling, grounded, and balanced; Grandma Freda, whose wisdom and vision have guided us since day one; and all other family members.

We wish to thank our many wonderful friends and co-workers for their encouragement and appreciation of our twin relationship; the special people at Running Press who helped transform this project from dream to a reality, and to our agent, Dick Croy.

Finally, a heartfelt thanks to the extraordinary people in this book.

—RDS and RDS

My greatest thanks go to the wonderful twins who allowed me to take their portraits.

—DF

Contents

60	**Jim Lewis**
	Jim Springer
64	**Jacqueline Hennessy**
	Jill Hennessy
70	**Raymond Brandt**
	Robert Brandt
72	**Jeff Wang**
	Julie Wang
76	**Nautica Sereno**
	Quincy Sereno
78	**Betsy McCagg**
	Mary McCagg
84	**Kelley Tesfaye**
	Maze Tesfaye

12

I really want John and Joseph to have an American Indian background because the Indian heritage is dying, and so many Indians are disappearing.

Eagle La Chappa, father of John and Joseph of the Kumeyaay Indian tribe, in which twins have always been considered a blessing, a sign of good luck and prosperity.

13

John Reiff

The best thing about being a twin is the deep friendship and the closeness. If I couldn't be with my brother and help him on the farm, I wouldn't be satisfied or happy. You always know that you have somebody to work with or back you up. That's the whole thing of being twins.

16

I wouldn't marry any woman if she wouldn't let me be with my brother when I wanted to. I just wouldn't have it.

Bill Reiff

The only thing we don't like is when people compare us competitively. 'Well, genetically you have the same potential, because you're twins. So how come she got an A and you got a C?'... We're best friends even though we fight a lot. Many people don't see that part . . . that there are struggles.

Our psychology teacher said that she sees an interpersonal dependency. She claims that everything's a joint decision. We agree on most things, but it's still my own opinion. It's not because we're trying to mold ourselves after each other.

MyLe Zagorsky

Kurt Froman,
on dancing with
twin Kyle for the
New York City Ballet

Twins are kind of bonded subconsciously. When you look at tapes of us dancing, we might be on different sides of the stage, but if you unfocus your eyes, it's like two people moving exactly the same.

We have finally realized that we can be individuals, thinking our own thoughts and forming our own opinions. We've never been closer.

Kyle Froman

I like when people make an effort to recognize 'these are your traits and these are his.' Especially since we're doing the same thing every day and working so hard to build a professional reputation for ourselves individually. Our personalities are very different. That's how most people tell us apart.

27

It's hard to explain to other people that Rasheda is not like a regular sister. She's closer because she's like half of me. I love my other siblings dearly, but it's not the same. If Rasheda's not there, something's missing.

Jamillah, twin to Rasheda (daughters of boxing champion, Muhammed Ali)

29

The only disadvantage of our twinship is the fear of something happening to Jamillah. When you love someone so much, it's devastating to think about it.

31

People used to give **us** the
same gifts or one to split.
They used to get us one
birthday card: 'Happy Birthday
twins', not Rasheda and Jamillah.
It makes you say, 'Hey, we're
two different people.'

Rasheda Ali-Walsh

I f Sean had a disability, I would be there for him, try to understand, and educate myself about it. Twins always have someone to say, 'Look, I'm here to care about you. Whatever your struggle, however you decide to deal with it. It might take you five years to get over this, but guess what? I'll be there in three years. I'll be there in five. I'll be there for as long as it takes.'

36

When the accident first happened, I was left with a sense of emptiness, of not being able to contribute or help. That really got to me because I went from doing everything with Scot to—boom—I couldn't do a single thing with him.

Sean Hollonbeck, inspired by Scot to become a physician

had no idea what to expect.
I thought, 'How wonderful,
two for the price of one.'
But it's more like having three.
The fact that they were born
at the same time is remarkable
and special, but they're also
both special in their own right,
whether they are twins or not.

40

I have double love every morning and every night when I get kissed goodnight. At night, when we have the baby monitor on, they talk for a long time in a language that only they understand.

James Keach, father of
John and Kristopher and
husband to Jane Seymour

Scott (and Mark)
Kelly, first identical
twins in history to be
selected for NASA's
astronaut corps

The Navy didn't even
know we were twins
until we showed up
on the same day for train-
ing at test pilot school.

When I heard that Scott was accepted (into the NASA class of 1996), I was almost as happy as when I found out that I made it! Not quite as much, but almost.

Mark Kelly

Jeannine Bobardt,
Denise's fraternal twin
sister and surrogate mother
to Denise's triplets.

I was given this gift of a healthy body and I just felt I had to share it. It wasn't Denise's fault that she ended up being sick. It could have been me.

48

We're pretty much like black and white. Brady's very artistic, into singing and dancing. And I love sports. And there's a fascination with our different sexual orientations and our being twins.

Brian Ralston

The challenge is trying to break down the perception that all twins are exactly the same. I think that challenge instantly goes away once people meet us, because they see how different we are, and how similar, too.

52

love telling people about my
brother. I always want my
friends to meet my other half.

Brian Ralston

Jeff Stanch, on his
experience of twins
marrying twins
and sharing a home
together. Ali and
Jeff Stanch and Cal
and Jim Stanch

We have our individuality
but we have the same
kind of commitment and
devotion to our marital relationship
as to our twins.

We're so close, that if one died, the other would probably have died of a broken heart. I couldn't picture life without him.

Brian McMullin, whose fraternal twin, Donald, was shot while they were on duty together as police officers.

Azra Kurtovic

Being twins really helped us get through the (Bosnian) war. . . . Whatever we face next, we know that there will always be somebody there for us.

It's great to be twins, *blizankinjes*, as they called us in Bosnian. I have somebody to talk to, somebody who knows me, a best friend.

Amina Kurtovic

60

I t was kind of like standing there and looking at myself. It wasn't like meeting a stranger. It felt great—like someone I hadn't seen for a long time.

Jim Springer after meeting his twin brother (also named Jim) for the first time in 39 years.

We were so close on the
tests (for the Minnesota
Study of Twins Reared
Apart) that we had to do them
over again because Dr. Bouchard
was afraid that if we didn't, nobody
was going to believe the results.
They would think we copied off
each other, even though we were
isolated in separate booths!

64

I think it's such a unique human experience to have somebody who is your soulmate. It's the closest equivalent you can have to somebody walking the earth who you know will always be there for you and understand you. The twin relationship is a microcosm of the whole human experience of intimacy.

Jill Hennessy

came out three minutes earlier and was skinny as a rake. Jill was nice and plump. That woman was monopolizing all the food in the womb!

We're strong opponents of twinsploitation. Which is the dehumanizing portrayal of twins on TV or in film in which they are rendered into this single entity that isn't whole unless the two are together.

Jill Hennessy

Raymond Brandt
whose twin Robert died
at age 20, prompting
Raymond to develop the
Twinless Twin Support
Group in his honor.

The first step is recognizing that you are still a twin. I've now had forty-seven years of separateness from Robert. I would not trade those twenty years for those forty-seven. Never. One moment of twinship is worth a lifetime.

We feel lucky to be boy-girl twins rather than identical or same-sex twins because it's not like looking in a mirror and constantly being compared. As long as I live, there will always be someone who started at the same exact time and the same exact place. I feel that I will always have a friend who's living a parallel life to mine, even though she's a girl and I'm a guy.

Jeff Wang

Julie Wang

The big thing about being twins is that we're peers— the same age group. It's not like he's older and therefore I have to listen to him, or I'm older and he has to do what I say. But it works both ways. We feel lucky to have an unconditional, lifelong friend.

They learned to say, 'It's my turn now' about a year ago. Nautica, who's the second-born, once asked me, 'Mommy, when can I be first-born?'

Drisana Sereno,
single mother of twin sons
Nautica and Quincy

Mary McCagg

On the water we're known almost as much for our fighting as for our speed. However, we prefer to label them 'verbal exchanges at high volume.'

We are always sisters and friends once practice is over.

Betsy McCagg, discussing their Olympic rowing careers

Our coach would yell, 'Come on, you're twins! Why don't you row like twins?' Yet, whenever the scrutiny was almost too much to bear, I knew I always had my sister fighting alongside me and rooting for me. I would not have survived if I hadn't had my sister to complain to, laugh with, cry to, and commiserate with.

Mary McCagg

I don't know if we can do this just because we've been with each other so much, or if there's actually some unique 'twin speak' occurring, but it has done a good job of perpetuating the twin myth on our team.

Maze Tesfaye

Our husbands got jealous because Kelley and I care so much about each other.

But my relationship with Maze and my relationship with my husband were not the same. They were different.

Kelley, co-owner with
Maze of the Twins Lounge
in Washington D.C.

Dr. Ralph Mendez who, along with his twin brother, Dr. Robert Mendez, is part of a team of physicians at the forefront of kidney transplantation.

When we operate together, it's sort of automatic. We can go through a whole surgery and not say a word. It's just like four hands out of the same brain.

When guys can't tell us apart or say, 'I'll take both of you,' I say, 'Excuse me, I don't think so! We're different people!' Or, if I go out with somebody and we break up and he tries to ask Tamera out, that's a big no-no.

Tia Mowry, with sister
Tamera, actresses on the
sitcom *Sister Sister*.

The biggest challenge of being twins is having people see you as individuals. Many times we wouldn't get acting jobs because we were twins. They didn't want to upset the one who wasn't chosen. One time they put our pictures face down and just chose one. That really hurt our feelings because we are two different people.

We see ourselves as a team, like Lucy and Ethel. We were never jealous of one another. Being twins is a gift from God.

Tamera Mowry

Joseph Fisch, describing
how the bond between
he and Boris helped them
survive the Holocaust.

Even in the worst times
twins still hold together.
That's why we're still
alive today. Boris and I always
helped each other. My father
told us, 'My boys, my twins,
you'll always be together. Help
each other. Never separate from
each other. That is my wish.'

אנכי יהוה
לא יהיה
לא תשא
זכור את
כבד את
לא תרצח
לא תנאף
לא תגנב
לא תענה
לא תחמד

We were determined to survive. We told each other, 'We will go back home, we will not die here, and we will fight for our lives.' There is no such thing that you are alone. God is always with you.

Boris Fisch

Patty Hensel, mother
of conjoined twins
Abigail and Brittany

If they had to be
put together, I
think they were put
together perfectly.

When people ask us, 'What's it like to be a twin?' We respond, 'Well, what's it like not to be a twin?' You can't describe it. I don't know any other way of life. I don't think there's anything more extraordinary about twins, to be honest with you. It's just different, it's a miracle of life, it's what God gave us.

Mario Andretti

There was always the wish, 'I'm capable of doing that, I wish it would have been me.' It's a little bittersweet. I loved for him to do well. I just wished it was me!

104

When we were on the track at the same time, you're darn right we were competitive. To me, he was just another faceless competitor. I wanted to beat him as much as he wanted to beat me. But that's natural. It's a good type of competition, not a negative competition.

Mario Andretti

Claudia Jefferson Beckman,
after sensing that Colleen,
miles away, had collided
with a semi-truck.

All of a sudden I felt an uneasiness, so I called home and told my mom, 'Colleen's been in a car accident.' Right after I hung up, the police called my parents and told them what had happened. Colleen was shaken up but was all right.

You know, we went through very rough times. We went through three wars and the Depression. But we've always kept our chins up and we've always made it. We love each other dearly. Everybody says we don't know how lucky we are, but we do!

Minerva Lipp, twin to
Marion Bartholomew
(now 96 years old)

This book has been
bound using handcraft
methods, and Smyth-sewn
to ensure durability.

The interior was designed by
Frances J. Soo Ping Chow.

The text was edited by Molly Jay.

The text was set in Frutiger
and Perpetua.